C000143623

A

1 Add together forty-seven and fifty-six.

2 The sum of two numbers is 89. If one i
   what is the other?

3 What is seven less than 9 × 8?

4 If three times a number is 63, what is the number?

5 Double the difference between 59 and 92.

6 Multiply 4.1 by 10.

7 Write these in order, smallest first:
   0.7, 2.0, 0.2, 1.25.

8 Add together 2.50 and 3.05.

9 Write 16-tenths as a decimal.

10 Add £1.05 + 80p + £2.25.

B

11 Which of these angles is acute?
    105°, 16°, 112°, 270°.

> Any angle less than 90° is an acute angle.

12 Write 7:15 p.m. as shown on the 24-hour clock.

13 What is the next number?   1, 4, 9, 16, ?

14 How much is ⅖ of £3?

15 Which of these is a prime number?
    89, 90, 91, 92, 93.

> 17 is a prime number. It has only 1 and itself as factors.

16 A packet of tea weighs 450 g. How many kilograms
    will 4 packets weigh?

17 If handkerchiefs cost 28p each, how much will
    seven handkerchiefs cost?

18 The perimeter of a rectangle is 8 cm. If it is 3 cm
    long, how wide is it?

19 How many weeks would it take to save £5 at a
    rate of 20p a week?

20 If 7 is added to a quarter of a certain number,
    the answer is 10. What is the number?

A

1 What is the total of fifty-eight and thirty-three?

2 Find the difference between 81 and 46.

3 What number is 14 more than 5×9?

4 Tins of beans are put into boxes, 20 tins to a box. How many boxes can be filled with 180 tins of beans?

5 Add seventeen to the difference between 9 and 14.

6 Divide 30.7 by 10.

7 Write these in order, smallest first: 1.50, 1.05, 5.01, 2.02.

8 Take 3.5 from 7.6.

9 Add together 1.90 and 7.06.

10 £1.07 $\times$ 10.

> In decimals $0 \cdot 3 = \frac{3}{10}$, $0 \cdot 03 = \frac{3}{100}$. ($0 \cdot 03$ means no tenths, but 3 hundredths.)

B

11 What is 9:35 p.m. as shown on the 24-hour clock?

12 What is the area of a rectangle 3 cm long and 9 cm wide?

> 1 square centimetre or 1 cm²

13 What is the average of 13, 9 and 8?

14 How many days are there altogether in March, April and May?

15 Is 59 a prime number?

16 Mrs Jackson was 25 minutes late to catch a train which was due at 16:45. At what time did she arrive at the station?

17 What fraction of 2 kg is 250 g?

18 Kevin cycles 20 metres in 6 seconds. How far would he go in one minute?

19 I spent 60p on buying an equal number of apples and oranges. Apples cost 8p each, and oranges 12p. How many oranges did I buy?

20 The distance round the school field is 250 metres. How many times should runners go round the field in order to complete ¾ km?

Task 3

A

1. What is the sum of twenty, forty-five and fifteen?
2. What is the difference between 33 and 62?

   When you multiply two numbers together you get a product.

3. Take 16 from the product of 8 and 6.
4. Five times a number is 85. What is the number?
5. Rulers cost 25p each. How much will 6 cost?
6. Write these in order, smallest first:
   0.13,   0.09,   0.3.

   0·4 > 0·05
   4 tenths is greater than 5 hundredths.

7. What amount of money is one hundred times bigger than £0.45?
8. Multiply 1.23 by 10.
9. Add together 3.4 and 6.
10. Divide £14.50 by 10.

B

11. What is ½ of £2.50 added to ¼ of £3?
12. What is 14:30 as shown on a 12-hour clock face?
13. What is the next number?   71,   66,   60,   53,   ?
14. Add 1¾ + 1½.

    The distance around the edge of a shape is the perimeter

15. A rectangle is 9 cm long and 5 cm wide. What is its perimeter?
16. Which is bigger in area, a square field 40 m each side, or a rectangular field, 30 m long and 50 m wide?
17. A kilogram loaf is cut into 25 equal slices. How heavy are 5 slices?
18. Three oranges cost 40p. How much would 15 oranges cost?
19. A bag contained an equal number of 10p pieces and 20p pieces. If the amount of money in the bag was £6, how many coins were there of each kind?
20. A man was 27 years old in 1982. How old will he be in the year 2000?

Triangle Matching

Match each triangle from set A with one from set B,
then divide the bigger number by the smaller one.

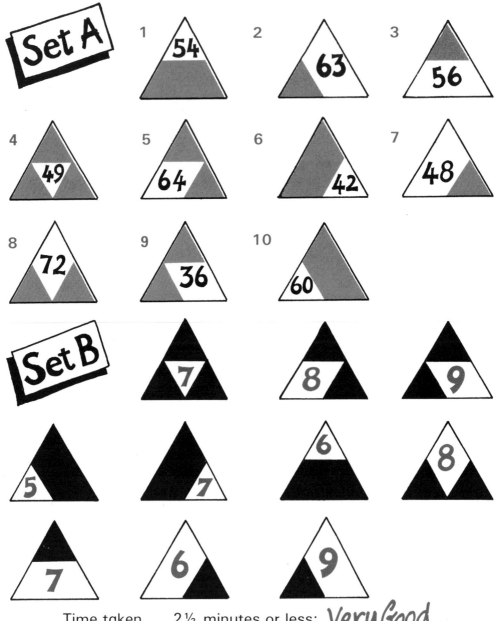

Time taken   2½ minutes or less: *Very Good*

3 minutes: *Good*

Task 4

A

1 Add together fifteen, twenty-seven and forty-five.

2 Two numbers add up to 74. If one of the numbers is 39, what is the other?

3 How much is 14p added to seven lots of 9p?

4 Divide 306 by 6.

5 What is fifteen less than 6×9?

6 Write $\frac{8}{100}$ as a decimal. ○

> $\frac{1}{100}$ = one hundredth
> = 0·01

7 Write $\frac{17}{10}$ as a decimal.

8 Divide 31.7 by 10.

9 Multiply 1.76 by 100.

10 £1.25 $\times$ 10 $\times$ 10.

B

11 What is half of ¾ ?

12 A lady spends 50p a day feeding her cat. How much would she spend for the month of June?

13 Write 9:15 a.m. as shown on the 24-hour clock.

14 How many degrees are there in ⅓ of a right-angle?

> cuboid

2cm

2cm

4 cm

> Volume
> = 2cm x 2cm x 4cm
> = 16cm^3

> 16 cubic centimetres

15 What is the volume of a cuboid 6 cm by 2 cm by 2 cm? ○

16 A family left for a fortnight's holiday on 27th July. On what date did they return?

17 50 pencils cost £3. How much would 8 pencils cost?

18 £¾ + £$\frac{1}{20}$ + £$\frac{1}{10}$.

19 What fraction of £8 is 50p?

20 Four times a number has the same value as the difference between 9 and 21. What is the number?

7

Task 5

1 Add together 14, thirty-six and twenty-three.

2 Take thirty-five from 81.

3 What is 13 less than 8 × 9?

4 How many five-a-side teams can be made from two classes of 35 children?

5 A shirt needs seven buttons down the front and one for each cuff. How many buttons are required for 20 shirts?

6 Multiply 3.01 by 100.

7 Put these in order, smallest first: 0.53,   1.76,   0.8.

8 What is the total weight of ten parcels each weighing 1.35 kg?

9 Multiply 5.3 by 10.

10 Which of these means 7 hundredths?
0.7,   0.77,   7.0,   0.07,   0.70.

11 What is the lowest common multiple of 6 and 8?

> 3 and 5 divide exactly into 15. So 15 is a *multiple* of 3 and a *multiple* of 5.

12 How many days are there altogether in the last three months of the year?

13 Add 2¾ to 3½.

14 What is the remainder when 495 is divided by 7?

15 What is the average of 16, 29 and 15?

16 A jar of fruit holds 400 g. How many jars could be filled from 2 kg of fruit?

17 In 4 weeks, Mum spent a total of £9.16 on newspapers. How much is this for each week?

18 A train travels at 88 km per hour. How far will it go in ¾ hour?

19 A bath fills at the rate of 5 litres a minute. How many litres will there be in the bath after 6½ minutes?

20 An ice-cream salesman has four flavours: strawberry, vanilla, chocolate and mint. How many different two-flavour ice-creams can he make?

Task 6

A

1 Find the sum of 13, 21 and fifty-six.

2 If two numbers add up to 115 and one of them is 57, what is the other?

3 Double the difference between 49 and 88.

4 How many 2½ cm strips can be cut from a piece of card 25 cm wide?

5 Four times a number is two less than 30. What is the number?

6 Divide 42.5 by 10.

7 How many centimetres are there in 27 mm?

8 Put these in order, greatest first: 7.4, 7.39, 7.17, 7.3.

10mm = 1 centimetre

9 Multiply $3^2 \times 10^2$.

10 What is one-tenth of a million?

B

11 What is the area of a rectangle 5 cm by 8 cm?

12 Is 37 a prime number?

13 Write 21:40, using a.m. or p.m, as shown on a 12-hour clock.

14 Debbie has 15 conkers, Bob has 20 conkers and Alan has 19 conkers. What is the average number of conkers for each child?

15 Which of these angles is a reflex angle? 24°, 124°, 78°, 224°.

An angle larger than 180° is called a reflex angle

16 A farmer owns 32 hens. 24 of them are white. What fraction of the hens are *not* white?

17 Take ³⁄₅ of £1 from ³⁄₁₀ of £2.

18 If a woman earns £400 in five weeks, how much does she earn in 6 weeks?

19 How many hours are there in ½ of 300 minutes?

20 If I am fifteen minutes early for my bus which is due at five past three, at what time do I arrive?

Task 7

1 What is the total of twenty-three, 51 and 29?

2 Find the difference between 130 and 24.

3 How many sixes are equal to double 27?

4 In a new restaurant, four chairs are needed for every table. If there are 17 tables, how many chairs are required?

5 Add nineteen to the product of 4 and 32.

6 Write 79 centimetres in metres.

7 100 sheets of 6 mm thick plywood are stacked in a pile. How many centimetres thick is the pile?

8 £1.75 × 100.

9 Write these in order, smallest first:
1.07, 2.9, 4.74, 3.67.

10 Divide three thousand by 10.

Length multiplied by width gives the AREA.

B

11 What is the area of a square with each side 7 cm long?

12 Take 3½ from 6¼.

13 What is the average of 7 cm, 9 cm and 5 cm?

14 What is ¹/₁₀ of £23?

15 What is 3:30 p.m. as shown on the 24-hour clock?

16 On a coach trip, children may travel at half price. How much does it cost altogether for Mr and Mrs Miles and their 3 children to travel, if the adult fare is £3?

17 If I travel 5 km in 10 minutes, how far will I go in one hour?

18 Beans cost a grocer 21p a tin. How much profit will she make on a box of 30 tins if she sells them at 27p each?

19 A metre ribbon is cut into 20 equal strips. How long would four of these strips measure?

20 Five times a number has the same value as twenty-eight added to seventeen. What is the number?

TRIANGLES

How many triangles are there altogether in each drawing?

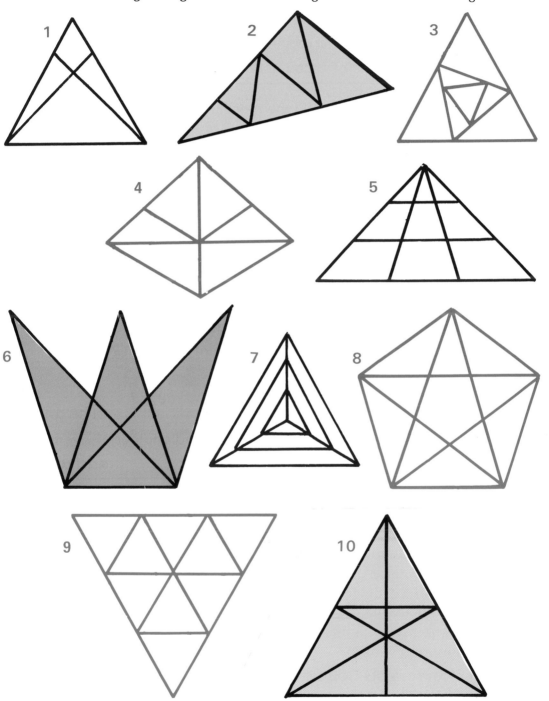

11

Task 8

A

1 What is the sum of thirty-seven, twenty-three and 59?

2 What is the difference between 143 and twenty-nine?

3 Double the sum of thirty-nine and twenty-three.

4 How many teams of 8 can you make from 3 classes of 32 children?

5 Find the number which is one more than half the product of 12 and 9.

6 Express 360 mm in metres.

7 Write 0.4 as a simple fraction in its lowest terms.

8 Ten boxes of chocolates cost £27.50. What is the cost of one box?

9 Multiply by 10 the smallest number here:
1.07,   0.9,   1.71,   1.06.

10 3.5×10^2.

$0.6 = \frac{6}{10}$. In its lowest terms $\frac{6}{10}$ becomes $\frac{3}{5}$

B

11 What is 11:15 p.m. as shown on the 24-hour clock?

12 What is the lowest common multiple of 16 and 12?

13 £½ + £¼ + £¾.

14 What is the next number?   2,   9,   18,   29,   ?

15 If a triangle contains an angle of 35° and another of 65°, what is the third angle?

The angles of a triangle add up to 180

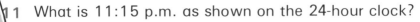

16 If 40 g of cheese costs 28p, how much will 60 g cost?

17 A goods train is travelling at 60 km per hour. How long will it take for the train driver to pass through a tunnel 2 km long?

18 A hammer costs twice as much as a screwdriver. Dad paid £6.60 for a hammer and a screwdriver. How much was the hammer?

19 What is the perimeter of a lawn 4.6 metres long and 2.4 metres wide?

20 If a comic costs 20p for a week, how much is that for a year?

A

1 Add together 25p, 47p and 38p.

2 What is the difference between £5.70 and £7.50?

3 Find half the sum of 37 and 65.

4 How many weeks are there in 56 days?

5 How many socks are needed altogether for 6 seven-a-side hockey teams?

6 Add 0.7 to five-tenths.

7 What is 49 ÷ 10?

8 Write **seventeen thousand, four hundred and six** in figures.

9 Put these in order, smallest first:
8.6,   6.27,   13.1,   5.03.

10 Multiply three-tenths by 100.

B

11 What is the lowest common multiple of 10 and 6?

12 What is half past five in the afternoon as shown on the 24-hour clock?

13 What is the value of 3^3?

2^3 means
$2 \times 2 \times 2$
$= 8.$

14 How many seconds are there in 4½ minutes?

15 What is the next number?   17,   26,   37,   50,   ?

16 What is the volume of a cuboid 4 cm × 3 cm × 5 cm?

17 One box holds 18 tins. How many boxes can be filled from a load of 90 tins?

18 A shopkeeper charged £3.81 instead of £3.18. How much did he overcharge?

19 How many degrees are there in a clockwise turn from south-east to south-west?

20 A picture and a frame together cost £4. If the picture costs £1 more than the frame, what is the cost of the picture?

Task 10

A

1. What is the total of 59p, 46p and 11p?
2. What is the difference between £4.55 and £9.00?
3. How many nines are equal to six dozen?
4. The product of two numbers is 75. If one of the numbers is 5, what is the other?
5. If 8 balloons cost 64p, what do nine balloons cost?
6. Write **15 032** in words.
7. How many 10p pieces are needed to make £20?
8. Write 1825 grams in kilograms.
9. Add 4.8 to five-tenths.
10. Multiply £1.05 by 100.

B

11. What is the date a fortnight after Christmas Day?
12. What is 25% of £20?

> 25% means ¼.

13. What is the next number?
    1½, 2¾, 4, 5¼, ?
14. How many quarters are there in 6 whole units?
15. What is the average of 39p, 43p and 38p?
16. How many degrees are there in an anticlockwise turn from north to east?
17. Find two whole numbers which have a sum of 51 and a difference of 7.
18. How many weeks would it take to save £7.50 at the rate of 25p per week?
19. One less than half of a number is 4. What is the number?
20. What is the volume of a cuboid 4 cm by 5 cm by 6 cm?

Consecutive numbers

1 What is the total of all of the odd numbers shown here?

2 Which of them are prime numbers?

3 Which number is a multiple of six?

4 Which two numbers have four as a factor?

5 Which three consecutive numbers add up to 66?

Numbers which follow immediately after each other are consecutive

Square numbers in a triangle

$5^2 = 25$. What is 8^2 worth?

$6^2 + 8^2 = \triangle^2$. What is $\triangle$ worth?

$1 + 3 + 5 = 3^2$.
(a) $1 + 3 + 5 + 7 = \triangle^2$. What is $\triangle$ worth?
(b) $1 + 3 + 5 + 7 + 9 = \bigcirc^2$. What is $\bigcirc$ worth?
(c) $1 + 3 + 5 + 7 + 9 + 11 + 13 = \square^2$. What is $\square$ worth?

Which two consecutive square numbers have a difference of
(a) 15,
(b) 17,
(c) 19?

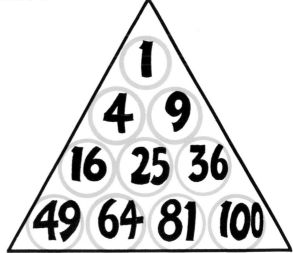

A

1 Add together 47 g, 39 g and 53 g.

2 What is 75 less than 165?

3 Subtract 69 from 94 and double the answer.

4 How much will eight pairs of socks cost at £1.20 per pair?

5 Take 20 from 500 and divide the answer by 8.

6 How many millimetres are in 12.5 cm?

7 What amount of money is one hundred times bigger than £0.62?

8 Take seven-tenths from 7.2.

9 2.34 + 0.2 + 1.3.
   Which of these is the correct answer?
   2.49,   38.4,   3.66,   3.84,   24.9.

10 Write **forty-three thousand and forty-three** in figures.

B

11 What is the value of 5^3?

12 Insert $>$ or $<$ or $=$ in $3\frac{1}{2} \times 10$ $5\frac{1}{2} \times 6$.

13 How many seconds are in one hour?

14 If one angle of a triangle is 45° and another is 65°, how big is the third angle?

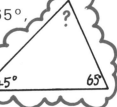

15 Write a quarter to nine in the evening as shown on the 24-hour clock.

16 What is the cost of 18 concert tickets at 25p each?

17 Wendy spent 30p on ice-cream, half as much on sweets, and twice as much on a magazine.
   How much did she spend altogether?

18 Five people share a taxi and the fare for the journey is £3.55. How much should each person pay?

19 What is the cost of 6 kg of carrots at 32p per kilo?

20 Three different coins together are worth 75p. What are they?

Task 12

A

1 What is the total of 48 cm, 32 cm and 59 cm?

2 From 209 take 4 × 12.

3 What is half the difference between 98 and 26?

4 Take 45 from 123.

5 If four notebooks cost £1.80, what do five notebooks cost?

6 How many millimetres are in 14.6 cm?

7 What is $\frac{6}{10}$ added to 0.75?

8 Multiply by 10 the greatest number here: 6.2, 4.75, 5.49, 7.05.

9 Write 1357 g in kilograms.

10 What is $\frac{1}{10}$ of £125?

B

11 If the radius of a circle is 3.5 cm, what is its diameter?

diameter
radius

12 What is the average of 15, 17, 19 and 21?

13 Which of these angles are obtuse?
34°, 134°, 234°, 334°.

An obtuse angle is greater than 90°, less than 180°.

14 How would you write a quarter to midnight on the 24-hour clock?

15 How many kilometres are in 6 × 250 metres?

16 How many 15p oranges can be bought for £1.20?

17 A man has £8. He spends ¼ of it and then gives £1.50 to his daughter. How much has he left?

18 One kilogram of oranges costs £1.20. What will ¾ kg cost?

19 Four times a certain number with two more added gives thirty. What is the number?

20 What is the cost of 10 metres of wire at 11p per ½ metre?

Task 13

1 What is the total of seventeen, forty-six and eighteen?

2 Subtract twenty-eight from 107.

3 Double the product of sixteen and three.

4 A packet contains 35 tissues. How many packets can be filled from 700 tissues?

5 What is six more than the difference between 27 and 49?

6 Write $11\frac{1}{10}$ as a decimal.

7 Multiply 4.3 by 100.

8 What is the difference between 7.3 and 9.65?

9 Add together 4.9 and five-tenths.

10 What is $\frac{3}{10}$ of 200?

11 The school netball team scored 12, 9, 11 and 8 in the last four matches. What was the average score?

12 Mrs Thompson spends 50p a day feeding her cat. How much does she spend on her cat during April?

13 Which is worth more, $\frac{2}{3}$ of £6 or $\frac{3}{4}$ of £6?

14 47% of the children in a school were boys. What percentage were girls?

15 What is 23:50 changed to a 12-hour clock time?

16 If 6 packets of sweets cost £3.60, how much do 4 similar packets of sweets cost?

17 The perimeter of a square is 320 mm. How long is each side of the square in cm?

18 A tank has 15 litres in it and it is $\frac{3}{5}$ full. How many litres does the tank hold when it is full?

19 $\frac{1}{4}$ of a piece of land is used for garages, $\frac{5}{8}$ for building flats and the rest for gardens. What fraction is used for gardens?

20 A certain number divided by seven gives one less than ten as the answer. What is the number?

4

HAROLD CLARKE
ROBERT SHEPHERD

CAMBRIDGE
UNIVERSITY PRESS

Designed and illustrated by Celia Hart
Cover design by Chris McLeod

PUBLISHED BY THE PRESS SYNDICATE OF THE UNIVERSITY OF CAMBRIDGE
The Pitt Building, Trumpington Street, Cambridge CB2 1RP, United Kingdom

CAMBRIDGE UNIVERSITY PRESS
The Edinburgh Building, Cambridge CB2 2RU, United Kingdom
40 West 20th Street, New York, NY 10011–4211, USA
10 Stamford Road, Oakleigh, Melbourne 3166, Australia

First published 1984
Tenth printing 1998

Printed in the United Kingdom at the University Press, Cambridge

Task 14

A

1 Add together 27, fifty-five and nineteen.

2 Two numbers add up to one hundred and seventeen. If one of them is 67, what is the other?

3 What is half the difference between 27 and 99?

4 If five times a number is double 40, what is the number?

5 Add nine to the product of 6 and 17.

6 Write $^{19}/_{10}$ as a decimal.

7 $0.4 \times 10 \times 10$.

8 Divide 13.7 by 10.

9 Write 375 centimetres in metres.

10 Add together fourteen-tenths and 3.1.

B

11 What is the volume of a cuboid 4 cm by 3½ cm by 2 cm?

12 The sum of two fractions is ⅞. If one of the fractions is ¼, what is the other?

13 What is 25% of £25?

14 What is the next number?   4,   9,   15,   22,   ?

15 In a school, 16% of the children cycle to school, 37% come by car or bus, and the rest walk What percentage of the children walk?

16 If 100 boxes of matches cost £7.50, what do 30 boxes cost?

17 A girl is one-fifth of her father's age and two years younger than her brother. If her father is 35 years old, how old is her brother?

18 A 50p piece weighs 13.5 g. How much does £5 worth of 50p pieces weigh?

19 A ruler and two pencils cost 28p. Two rulers and five pencils cost 64p. How much is one pencil?

20 The 2.15 p.m. train left 25 minutes late. What did the 24-hour clock say as the train left?

TWELVE FRACTIONS

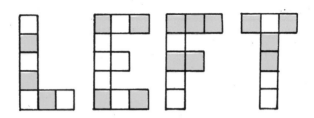

1 What fraction of the letter L is shaded?

2 What fraction of the letter E is shaded?
   How many fifths is this?

3 What fraction of the letter F is shaded?

4 What fraction of the letter T is shaded?

5 What fraction of the whole word LEFT is shaded?

What fraction of each of these shapes is shaded?

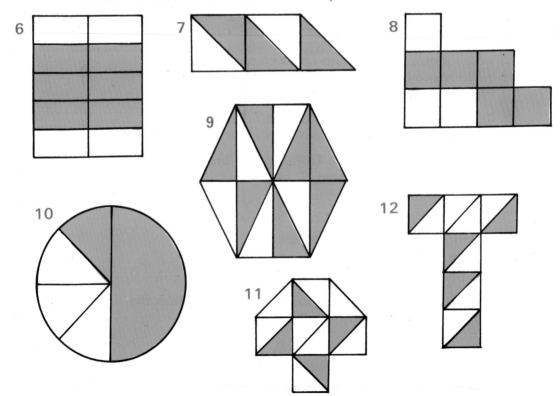

20

Task 15

A

1 Increase the total of 48 and 19 by twenty-three.

2 Take 45 from one hundred and twenty-three.

3 What is fifteen less than the product of 3 and 25?

4 What is ¼ of 428?

5 How many boots will need cleaning when five eight-a-side rugby teams have finished their tournament?

6 £1.05 × 10 × 10.

7 Divide 176 by 10.

8 Write these in order, smallest first:
   3, 4.2, 2.4, 0.53, 5.3.

9 Multiply 8.3 by 100.

10 How many millimetres are there in 18.7 centimetres?

B

11 How many degrees does the minute hand of a clock turn when moving from 10:15 to 10:45?

12 What is the average of 15, 16, 19 and 22?

13 How many hours and minutes are there in 135 minutes?

14 If July 13th is a Wednesday, what day is July 22nd?

15 Which of these numbers is a prime number?
   39, 49, 59, 69.

16 Two knives cost £3. A knife and two forks cost £4. What does a fork cost?

17 Rows of seats are lettered from A to H. If there are 15 seats in a row, how many seats are there altogether?

18 Emma's bedroom is 3.25 metres long and 2.75 metres wide. What is the perimeter of the room?

19 A one litre can is $\frac{9}{10}$ full. How many millilitres can still be poured in?

20 What number is halfway between 23 and 41?

Task 16

1. What is the sum of 6^2 and 4×11?
2. What is the difference between 141 and eighty-six?
3. Find the value of $(3 \times 8) + (7 \times 8)$.
4. Share £3.52 by 8.
5. Add twenty-four to the product of 24 and 9.
6. 6.3×10^2.
7. Take three-tenths from 5.1.
8. Divide 334 by 10.
9. Add $3\frac{6}{10}$ to $1\frac{1}{2}$.
10. Take the smallest from the largest here:
    2.7,   0.7,   4.1,   6.

11. Is 163 a multiple of 7?
12. Which of these angles is acute?
    $160°$, $70°$, $105°$, $210°$.
13. $\frac{5}{6} + \frac{5}{6} + \frac{5}{6}$.
14. Write a quarter to six in the afternoon as shown on the 24-hour clock.
15. Find the perimeter of a square which has an area of 49 cm^2.
16. A train journey starts at 9.45 a.m. If the journey takes 3 hours 40 minutes, when does the train arrive?
17. Julie has £5 and Jason has half that amount. If Robert has $\frac{1}{5}$ of what Jason has, how much have they altogether?
18. If June 1st is a Sunday what day will July 1st be?
19. To make four sandwiches Mum needed bread (27p), ham (35p) and butter (18p). What was the cost of each sandwich?
20. 2.700 kg of jam were poured equally into 6 jars. How many grams were put into each jar?

22

1 Find the sum of 23, twenty-eight and 27.

2 Take fifty-seven from 113.

3 How many boots will be worn by 6 rows of soldiers, when each row contains 15 soldiers?

4 How many boxes can be filled from 840 matches if 40 matches are put in each box?

5 Double the difference between 48 and 67.

6 Divide £30.10 by 10.

7 How many metres are in 3.45 kilometres?

8 Add together 0.3, five-tenths and 2.6.

9 Multiply 0.45 by 1000.

10 How many 20p coins are needed to make £30?

11 How many lines of symmetry has an equilateral triangle?

12 Find the highest common factor of 81 and 36.

13 What is the perimeter of an equilateral triangle with each side 5½ cm long?

equilateral triangle

14 What is the next number?   48,   39,   28,   15,   ?

15 Put $>$ or $<$ or $=$ in 4½ $\times$ 7 $\square$ 3½ $\times$ 9.

16 If 5 boxes of eggs cost £2.95, how much will 2 cost?

17 A car uses 8 litres of petrol for a journey of 80 km. How much petrol is needed for a 100 km journey?

18 Six apples and two oranges cost 70p. An apple and an orange cost 19p. How much is one orange?

19 A football match kicked off at 3:15 p.m. The final whistle blew at 4:57 p.m. How long did the match last?

20 If 3 cassettes cost £7.20, what would 5 similar cassettes cost?

1 How many litres are there altogether in four full
   bottles of brush cleaner?

2 How many tins of varnish are needed to make one litre?

3 How many millilitres are left in the small paint tin
   when one quarter of the paint has been used?

4 How many millilitres of paint are there altogether in
   two large tins of paint?

5 Does the varnish tin hold more than $\frac{3}{10}$ of a litre?

6 How many litres are needed to fill 10 tins of varnish?

7 Dad wishes to buy 5 litres of paint. How much cheaper
   is it to buy two 2½-litre tins than five 1-litre tins?

8 Mrs Parker bought a tin of varnish and a litre of paint.
   How much change did she get from a £5 note?

9 How many 250-ml bottles of brush cleaner can be
   filled from a tank containing 5 litres?

10 What is the difference in price between two litres of
   paint; and two tins of varnish and one paint brush?

A

1 What is the total of eighteen, 28 and 38?

2 Reduce 110 by 47.

3 What is half the product of five and twenty-six?

4 Share 408 by six.

5 If five times a number is 105, what is the number?

6 Write $\frac{5}{10}$ as a decimal.

7 Add together 2.4 and $\frac{3}{10}$.

8 If 10 bars of chocolate cost £5.50, what does one bar cost?

9 How many millimetres are there in 7.25 metres?

10 Multiply 0.7 by 10^3.

B

11 The base angles of an isosceles triangle are each 48°. What is the angle at the top of the triangle?

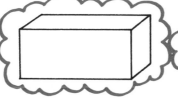

48° 49°
isosceles triangle

12 Take 3¾ from 6¼.

13 What is 50% of £7.20? **50% is one half.**

14 What is the next number?   13,   18,   25,   34,   ?

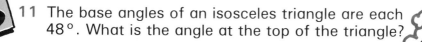

Volume = length × width × height

15 What is the volume of a cuboid 4 cm by 7½ cm by 2 cm?

16 Add together ¾ of £5 and ½ of £7.50.

17 If toffee bars cost 16p each, how much will 9 bars cost?

18 Tina is ¼ of her mother's age, but two years older than Dave. If Tina's mother is 36, how old is Dave?

19 From 1½ metres of ribbon a teacher has to cut 5 equal lengths. How long is each ribbon?

20 How much will 3.2 kg of potatoes cost at 20p a kilogram?

Task 19

A

1 Increase the total of 24 and sixteen by fifty-three.

2 What is forty-four less than 125?

3 What is twelve more than the product of 4 and 47?

4 What is one-third of 357?

5 Find the difference between 83 and 27, and then double it.

6 Multiply £0.35 by 100.

7 How many grams are there in 3.03 kg?

8 Multiply 0.04 by 10^3.

9 Write $^{67}/_{100}$ as a decimal.

10 How many 20p coins would be needed to make £25?

B

11 What is twenty-five minutes to four in the afternoon as shown on the 24-hour clock?

12 Find $^3/_5$ of 2 kg in grams.

13 $1\frac{1}{2} - \frac{5}{8}$.

14 What is 10% of 50 litres?

15 What is the next number?
1.5,   2.4,   3.4,   4.5,   ?

16 The train was ten minutes late. It arrived at 4 minutes after midnight. When was it due according to the 24-hour clock?

17 What is the cost of 20 boxes of fruit at £3.45 a box?

18 In a class of children, $^3/_5$ are boys. If there are ten girls in the class, how many children are there altogether?

19 Add 25% of £6 to 10% of £5.50.

20 What is the area of a rectangle 6 cm by 15 mm?

One litre = 1000 ml

10% means $\frac{1}{10}$

Task 20

A

1 Add together forty-four, twenty-two and nineteen.

2 What is the difference between eighty-six and 119?

3 What is the total of 3×27 and 7×27?

4 Take one from 400 and divide by seven.

5 Add sixteen to the product of 43 and 4.

6 How many kilograms are in 4750 grams?

7 Add ½ to $\frac{5}{100}$ and give the answer as a decimal.

8 Divide 37.5 by 10.

9 Write $\frac{114}{100}$ as a decimal.

10 Add $\frac{5}{100} + \frac{3}{10} + 1$, using decimals.

B

11 A triangle contains one angle of 65° and another of 25°. What is the third angle?

12 1.5×10^3.

13 What is 25% of 3 km?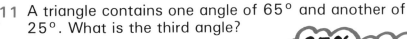

> 25% means $\frac{25}{100} = \frac{1}{4}$

14 How many grams are in 2½ lots of 3 kg?

15 What is the volume of a cube with each side 5 cm in length?

16 If three books cost £1.65, how much will 5 similar books cost?

17 I walked to town and it took me 75 minutes. I left home at ten minutes to 6 p.m., so when did I arrive in town?

18 1.5 kg of sweets is divided equally into 30 packets. What is the weight of each packet of sweets?

19 A one-litre bottle is already ¾ full. After 150 ml more has been poured in, how much is in the bottle?

20 Mum spends £2.80 and £4.50 at the shops on Tuesday. How much does she have left out of £10?

Task 21

A

1 What is the total of 63 cm, 35 cm and 27 cm?

2 From 720 take 125.

3 What is 4^2 added to twelve times seven?

4 What is ¼ of 256?

5 Add 15 to the product of 9 and 16.

6 Multiply 243 by 100.

7 Add 4.8 to $\frac{7}{10}$.

8 How many centimetres are there in 2.3 metres?

9 What is 10% of 270?

10 Add $\frac{7}{10}$ to $\frac{17}{100}$ and give the answer as a decimal.

B

11 Which of these angles is an acute angle?
110°, 245°, 85°, 135°.

regular hexagon

12 How many lines of symmetry has a regular hexagon?

13 Write 5 minutes to eight in the evening as shown on the 24-hour clock.

14 What is 10% of £25 added to 25% of £10.

15 What is the area of a rectangle 7½ cm long and 4 cm wide?

16 Three-quarters of Darren's money is 66p. How much has he altogether?

17 Susan is a quarter of her Dad's age, but 3 years older than her sister Helen. If Helen is 5 years old, how old is Dad?

18 A 50p piece weighs 13.5 g. In a bag are 50p pieces weighing 270 g. What is their total value?

19 I bought six plates costing 45p each. How much change did I receive from a £5 note?

20 A pear and a banana cost 21p. Three pears and two bananas cost 54p. What is the cost of a pear?

Number crunching

Numbers are fed into this machine as shown, then counted on. Say what the result would be in each case.

1. 13 + 8 3269
2. 15 + 25 1368
3. 150 + 150 6247
4. 40 + 25 4985
5. 62 + 44 52199
6. 92 + 42 23755
7. 80 + 46 7496
8. 37 + 87 5876

This time the machine adds or subtracts first of all, then it multiplies by 100. Say what the result would be in each case.

9. 17 + 19 × 100
10. 13 + 14 + 15 × 100
11. 52 − 25 × 100
12. 29 + 41 × 100
13. 23 + 24 + 25 × 100
14. 80 − 35 × 100
15. 53 − 17 × 100

Task 22

1 What is the total of 67p, 58p and 33p?

2 Two numbers add up to 116. If one of the numbers is 38, what is the other?

3 What is ⅓ of 405?

4 Double the difference between 58 and 85.

5 Toy cars are packed 24 to a box. How many boxes can be filled using 480 toy cars?

6 How much more than 367 ml is one litre?

7 Divide 38.7 by 10.

8 Subtract 555 g from 2 kg.

9 Add ten to 1897 and write the answer in words.

10 Write the answer to 125 ml × 10 in litres.

11 Insert > or < or = in 10 × 3½ ☐ 6 × 6½.

12 Which two of these angles add up to one right-angle? 33°, 36°, 47°, 54°, 67°.

13 Find the next number in this series:
3.9, 3.3, 2.7, 2.1

14 What is the perimeter of a regular pentagon with each side 7 cm?

15 Three angles of a quadrilateral are 70°, 100° and 110°. What is the fourth angle?

16 What is the difference in weight between five 210 g tins and one kilogram tin?

17 Five pens cost £1.35 altogether. What would 7 similar pens cost?

18 Rows of seats are lettered A to K. If each row contains 12 seats, how many seats are there altogether?

19 Anna spent £2.75, which was one quarter of her money. How much money did she have to start with?

20 How many 60 g bags of sweets can be made up from 1 ½ kg of sweets?

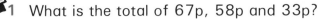

A regular pentagon has five regular sides

The angles of a quadrilateral add up to 360°.

A

1 What is the sum of 67 cm, 24 cm and 59 cm?

2 How many groups of six are there in 12 nines?

3 The sum of two numbers is 106. If one of the numbers is 49, what is the other?

4 Add 19 to the product of 23 and 4.

5 Add together 335 ml and 240 ml.

6 What is the value of $(7 \times 33) + (3 \times 33)$?

7 Take one hundred from 12 097 and write the answer in words.

8 Write these in order, smallest first:
0.36, $^{57}/_{100}$, $^{4}/_{10}$.

9 Divide 3.75 km by 10 and give the answer in metres.

10 Multiply 2½ metres by 10 and give the answer in centimetres.

B

11 What are the missing amounts?
£4.58, ☐ , £4.76, £4.85, ☐

12 Which is the odd one out in this set of fractions?
$^{2}/_{8}$, $^{1}/_{4}$, $^{3}/_{12}$, $^{1}/_{3}$.

13 A freezer is 1500 mm long. How many metres is this?

14 Which vowels have a vertical axis of symmetry?
A, E, I, O, U.

15 Which is the next prime number after 101?

16 The difference between ¼ and ½ of a certain number is 9. Find the number.

17 What change will be received from £5 after buying 7 packets of biscuits at 43p a packet?

18 There are five more boys than girls in a class of 31 children. How many boys are there in the class?

19 A car needs 10 litres of petrol to travel 120 km. How many litres would be needed for a journey of 180 km?

20 If 4th July was a Wednesday, on what day was 23rd June?

a
vertical
axis of
symmetry

A

1 Add together 58 mm, 44 mm and 37 mm.

2 What is 11 less than 5 × 18?

3 How many five-a-side teams can be made from four classes of 25?

4 Increase 5 dozen by 3 × 9.

5 How much will five shirts cost, if each shirt cost £4.50?

6 What is the difference between 450 grams and 1¼ kg?

7 How many millilitres are there in 0.25 litres?

8 What is 10% of £4.50?

9 Multiply £1.39 by 100.

10 Add ⅕ to ¾, and write the result as a decimal.

> ⅕ is equivalent to ²⁄₁₀.

B

11 What is eleven minutes to five in the afternoon on the 24-hour clock?

12 What is the perimeter of a hexagon with each side 3½ cm long?

> A hexagon is a shape with six sides.

13 Insert > or = or < in 4½ × 5 ☐ 3½ × 7.

14 What is the volume of a cuboid 3 cm by 2 cm by 1½ cm?

15 What is the next number in this series?
2.4, 3.1, 3.8, 4.5, ?

16 Three angles of a quadrilateral are 105°, 95° and 75°. What is the fourth angle?

17 ⅗ of Keith's money is 72p. How much does Keith have altogether?

18 A journey started at 4:45 p.m. If it took 2¾ hours to complete, when did the journey finish?

19 In a class ³⁄₇ are boys. There are 16 girls in the class, so how many boys are there?

20 After facing south, a Guide turned 135° clockwise. Which compass direction was she now facing?

Links

Copy out each set of links.
Put in the missing numbers.

1. 8 — 15 — 22 — ☐ — ☐ — 43

2. 1/10 — 0·2 — 3/10 — 0·4 — ○ — ○

3. 1 — 3 — 9 — ◇ — ◇ — 243

4. 9·15 a.m. — 9·40 a.m. — ☐ — 10·30 a.m — ☐ — ☐

5. 2,500 — ☐ — 25 — 2·5 — ☐

Different sums, same answers

Find the two sums in each row which give the same answer.

	A	B	C	D	E
1	3 × 3	7 × 2	24 ÷ 6	½ of 16	36 ÷ 4
2	50/2	3 × 9	36 ÷ 3	41 − 14	16 + 10
3	17 + 18	4 × 9	64/2	7 × 5	50 − 12
4	26 + 21	60 − 11	9 × 7	54 ÷ 6	7^2
5	0·5 + 0·2	½ + ¼	1 − ⅛	0·25 × 3	3/10 + ½

Task 25

1 Increase the total of
   forty-two and one hundred and seven by 19.

2 The sum of two numbers is 139. One is 56.
   What is the other?

3 How many teams of six can you make from
   five dozen children?

4 Divide 1107 by 3.

5 Take 30 from 600 and divide the result by 5.

6 Take 100 from 21 063 and write the answer in words.

7 How many grams are there in 2.07 kilograms?

8 Multiply 43.64 by 10^3.

9 Take five-tenths from 2.4.

10 Write these in descending order:
   $^{47}/_{10}$, $^{24}/_{100}$, $^{115}/_{100}$.

Descending order means getting smaller.

11 Find the value of $2\frac{3}{4} + 3\frac{1}{8}$.

12 Which of these angles is obtuse?
   89°, 95°, 37°, 192°.

13 What is 25% of £7.20?

14 What is the average of 33p, 46p and 38p?

15 What is the perimeter of a square which has an
   area of 64 square centimetres?

16 What change will there be after paying for
   three 68p books with £5?

17 What is the total length of three pieces of
   wood 1.25 m, 2½ m and 75 cm long?

18 The journey home from Newcastle takes 3¼ hours.
   If it started at 10:35 a.m, when did I get home?

19 David and Nicola have 70p between them. If David
   has 20p more than Nicola, how much has David?

20 There are three vases on a shelf, one red, one blue
   and one green. In how many different ways could
   they be arranged to stand in a row?

A

1 Find the total of 67, 26 and one hundred and three.

2 What is 48 less than 121?

3 Bread rolls are packed four to a bag. How many bags can be filled from 12 dozen rolls?

4 $(2 \times 24) + (8 \times 24)$.

5 How many gloves are needed to keep the hands of seven dozen children warm?

6 Add 100 to 11 907 and write the answer in words.

7 Divide 420 by 10^2.

8 Add 1.7 to eleven-tenths.

9 Write **one hundred and fifty-six hundredths** as a decimal.

10 Which is smaller, 0.65 or $^{64}/_{100}$?

B

11 Which vowel has two lines of symmetry?
A, E, I, O, U.

12 What is the HCF of 81, 36 and 72?

> HCF → Highest Common Factor

13 What is the perimeter of a regular octagon of side 4½ cm?

14 Two angles in a triangle are 38° and 84°. What is the third angle?

15 Insert > or < or = in 4½ × 7 ☐ 3 × 10½.

16 If September 13th was a Tuesday, on what day was August 30th?

17 If one-third of my weight is 27.3 kilograms, how much do I weigh?

> An octagon is an eight sided shape.

18 If 16 is taken from a third of a number, the answer is 7. What is the number?

19 The perimeter of a rectangle is 34 cm. If it is 7 cm wide, what is its area?

20 A bucket holds 7 litres. How many 250 ml bottles can be filled from the bucket?

Task 27

A

1 Increase the total of 49 and 27 by eighty-three.

2 Two numbers add up to one hundred and sixteen. One is 39. What is the other?

3 Double the product of 16 and six.

4 What is $\frac{1}{8}$ of 512?

5 Four times a number has the same value as one-third of 96. What is the number?

6 Multiply 8.13 by 10^2.

7 Add $\frac{5}{10}$ to 2.7.

8 Write 407 mm in metres.

9 What is the difference between 0.68 and 1.29?

10 Multiply 3070 by ten and write the answer in words.

B

11 How would you write 12 minutes after midnight on the 24-hour clock?

12 25% of the seats were empty, but 90 seats were taken. How many empty seats were there?

13 How many degrees would I turn moving clockwise from north-west to east?

14 What is the next number in this series?
0.6,   1.3,   2.1,   3.0,   ?

15 Insert > or < or = in 6 × 9½ ◯ 9 × 6½.

16 A coat is reduced by 20%. It was £15. How much is it now?

17 The area of a rectangle is 48 cm². If it is 4 cm wide, what is its perimeter?

18 One tin of salmon weighs 650 grams. How many kilograms will five tins weigh?

19 A train travels at 75 km an hour. How far will it have travelled after twenty minutes?

20 A bat and ball cost £1.20. If the bat costs three times as much as the ball, how much does the bat cost?

Task 28

A

1　What is the sum of 59p, 27p and 33p?
　Write your answer in £.

2　What is the difference between £1.23 and 87p?

3　Toy cars are fitted with 4 wheels each. How many
　toy cars can be fitted using 608 wheels?

4　Five times a number is 8 less than the product of
　3 and sixteen. What is the number?

5　$(3 \times 19) + (7 \times 19)$.

6　Add together the two smallest numbers here:
　0.97,　0.78,　0.83,　0.79,　0.82.

7　Divide 838 by 10^2.

8　Multiply 37p by 200.

9　Take fifteen-hundredths from 6-tenths.
　Give the answer as a decimal.

10　Which is bigger, 6.17 or 97-hundredths?

B

11　Which of these angles is reflex?
　176°,　76°,　276°,　6°.

12　What is the value of $4\frac{3}{8} - 3\frac{1}{2}$?

13　Which is the next prime number greater than 79?

14　What is the LCM of 2, 5 and 7? **LCM means Lowest Common Multiple**

15　Write seventeen minutes to midnight as shown
　on the 24-hour clock.

16　If May 10th was on a Sunday, on what day was
　April 26th?

17　⅘ of the class are going on an outing, but six are
　staying behind. How many are there in the class?

18　If three ties cost £4.17, how much will 5 cost?

19　The area of a rectangle is 54 cm². Its perimeter is
　30 cm. What is the length of the rectangle?

20　A tank contains 9 litres. How many 200 ml bottles
　can be filled from half of the tank?

Strip A + Strip C will measure 11 centimetres.
Which strips are needed to measure these lengths?
(Use two or three strips, but not the same strip twice.)

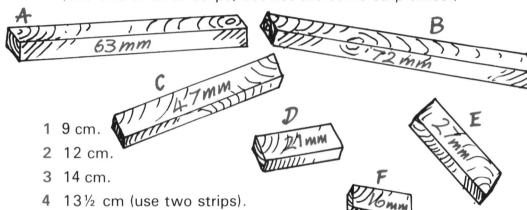

1 9 cm.

2 12 cm.

3 14 cm.

4 13½ cm (use two strips).

5 13½ cm (use three strips).

6 How many strip Bs would be needed to make a
length of 36 centimetres?

1 This magic square adds up
to £3.00 in each direction.
Copy the square and fill in
each missing amount.

£1·60		
60p		
	£1·80	40p

2 The value of each row, column
and diagonal is the same.
Copy and complete it.

1·5		1·1
	0·9	
		0·3

3 This magic square adds up
to 48 in each direction.
Copy and complete it.

14		18
15		

4 Use 30, 60, 90 and 100 to
complete this. Each row should
then add up to 200.

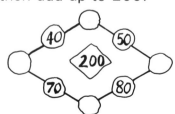

Task 29

A

1   Add together 39 cm, 42 cm and 28 cm.

2   The sum of two numbers is 159. One is 86. What is the other?

3   Five times a number is 185. What is the number?

4   Share £4.97 by seven.

5   Add 47 to the product of 16 and 9.

6   What is the value of a million divided by 100?

7   Multiply 2.34 by 10^3.

> Ascending means growing larger.

8   Write these in ascending order: $^{32}/_{10}$, $^{315}/_{100}$,   0.37.

9   Write **one hundred and twenty-two tenths** as a decimal.

10   Subtract the smallest number from the largest here:

   0.38,   0.41,   0.82,   0.57.

B

11   One of the base angles of an isosceles triangle is 36°. What is the angle at the top?

> isosceles triangle

12   What is the average of 3.3 kg, 2.9 kg and 2.2 kg?

13   Insert < or > or = in 8 × 6½ ◯ 13 × 4.

14   What is the perimeter of a regular octagon of side 15 cm?

15   Is 11 a prime factor of 1078?

16   The area of a rectangle is 84 cm². It is 14 cm long. What is its perimeter?

17   I can fill 3 glasses from 500 ml of milk. How many glasses can I fill from 2 litres of milk?

18   A lorry travelled for 40 minutes at 66 km an hour. How far did it travel?

19   Packets of sweets cost a man 13p each. He resells them at 20p each. How much profit will he make if he sells 200 packets?

20   Double a number has the same value as three times the square of six. What is the number?

Task 30

1. What is the total of 41 mm, 38 mm and 26 mm?

2. Take 62 from 132.

3. Double the difference between (5 × 9) and fifteen lots of eight.

4. What is $\frac{1}{5}$ of 3005?

5. Three times a number is equal to half the difference between 18 and 42. What is the number?

6. Write these in descending order: $\frac{87}{100}$, 0.25, $\frac{13}{10}$.

7. What is the difference between 8.1 seconds and 4.05 seconds?

8. Divide 317 by 10^2.

9. If a pile of ten identical bricks reaches a height of 75 cm, how high is each brick?

10. Take eighteen-tenths from 3.7.

11. What is $\frac{5}{10}$ of 500?

12. What is the next number?
    2.7, 3.2, 4.0, 5.1, ?

13. What is 25% of £3.60 + 50% of £5.00?

14. What is the LCM of 3, 8 and 12?

15. The top angle of an isosceles triangle is 86°. What are the base angles?

16. If I start by facing east and then turn clockwise 135°, in which direction do I finish?

17. A 3-kg cheese is cut into 150 g pieces and sold at 60p a piece. How much money is taken?

18. A bottle of pop contains 250 ml. How many litres are there altogether in 22 bottles?

19. What is the cost of 9 pencils at 13p each and six rubbers at 11p each?

20. If July 12th is a Friday, on what day does August 1st fall?